THE LITTLE GREEK ALPHABET BOOK

THE LITTLE GREEK ALPHABET BOOK

by Ennis Rees

Designed and illustrated by George Salter

Prentice-Hall, Inc.   Englewood Cliffs, N. J.

The LITTLE GREEK ALPHABET BOOK by Ennis Rees

Library of Congress Catalog Card Number: 68-18935

Prentice-Hall International, Inc., London
Prentice-Hall of Australia, Pty., Ltd., Sydney
Prentice-Hall of Canada, Ltd., Toronto
Prentice-Hall of India Private Ltd., New Delhi
Prentice-Hall of Japan, Inc., Tokyo

With silver and gold

And Phoenician antiques

The alphabet

Was brought to the Greeks,

Who greatly improved it

And passed it thus

To the Romans

And to us.

V U V U

VV W

J

Naturally

Some changes occurred

In the letters

Of a word,

So that the alpha-

bet we know

Is different from that

Of long ago.

Here, then, you'll see

The alphabet

As the Greeks once knew it

And know it yet,

And when you have seen

How their alphabet looks,

You may want to read

The great Greek books.

α β γ δ
ε ζ η ϑ
ι κ λ μ
ν ξ ο π
ϱ σ ς τ υ
φ χ ψ ω

ALPHA is first

It's like our A.

Here it is written

The ancient Greek way.

ALPHA

alpha

11

BETA is B.

In the word *alpha-bet*,

Alpha and *beta*

Have happily met.

BETA   beta

Pronounce BAY'TA

13

GAMMA is Greek

For our letter G.

"What happened," you ask,

"To C and D?"

GAMMA   gamma

Гγ

C? D?

DELTA is D.

The C you're missing

Will turn up soon.

It's the *kind* in *kissing*.

DELTA   delta

17

EPSILON, yes —

It's the Greek word for E,

But short as in *jet,*

Not long as in gee.

EPSILON   epsilon

Pronounce EP'SILON

19

ZETA sounds

Like a bumblebee,

But in front of the Z

Sometimes there's a D.

ZETA   zeta

as in adze.

Ζ ζ

Pronounce DZAY'TA

ETA is used

As a kind of long E,

But it looks like an H.

Don't you agree?

ETA

eta

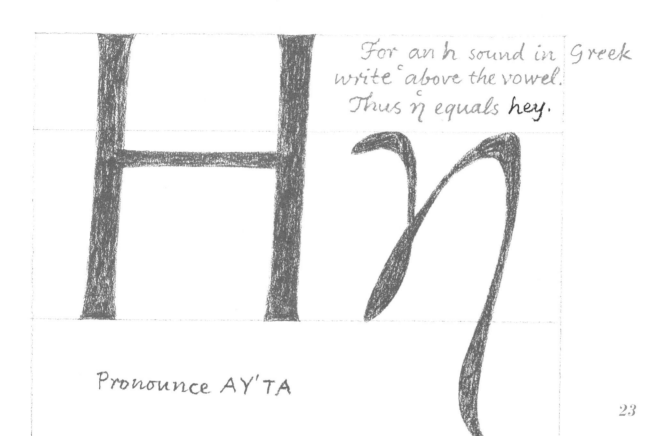

For an h sound in Greek
write ͨ above the vowel.
Thus ἡ equals **hey**.

Pronounce AY'TA

23

THETA, I guess,

Is what Zeta ate,

Or so the rhyme says

At any rate.

THETA   theta

ZETA ETA THETA.

Pronounce THAY'TA. Equals th.

25

IOTA is I,

And you will recall,

"Not one iota"

Means "nothing at all."

IOTA

iota

Pronounce EEO′ TA

27

KAPPA is made

Like our letter K

You know it already

So shout hooray!

KAPPA   kappa

29

LAMBDA is L.

Look at it and sigh.

It's an upside-down

Big V and small y.

LAMBDA

lambda

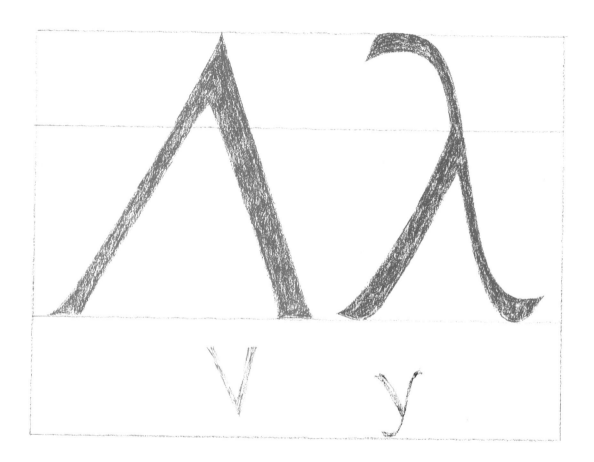

31

MU is like M,

And whenever cows speak,

They say it quite clearly

In classical Greek.

MU   mu

33

NU is N,

But that little v

Is the small way to write it.

Don't blame me!

NU   nu

35

XI has a sound

Like the x in *ax*,

Or if you prefer,

The *ks* in *quacks*.

XI

xi

Pronounce KSEE

OMICRON reads

Very much like a riddle,

Till you find the word means

"An o that is little."

OMICRON   omicron

That is, short. Pronounce O'MICRON

39

PI is our P,

And already you're able

To write it in Greek —

Like a tiny table.

PI

pi

Pronounce PEE

41

RHO is an R

with a little trill,

Which if you won't try,

A canary will.

RHO   rho

43

SIGMA, like S,

An old goose would miss,

If she didn't have it

When she tried to hiss.

SIGMA
sigma

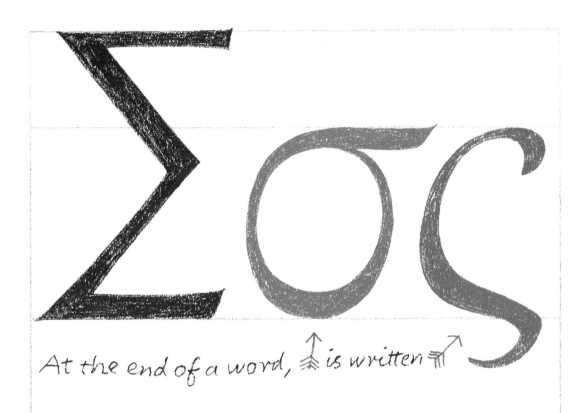

Σ ος

At the end of a word, ↑ is written ↗

TAU is for T.

It rhymes with bow wow.

If you say it three times,

You won't forget how.

TAU   tau

"T-OW!"

UPSILON serves

As the U in a word.

The capital looks

Like a long-legged bird.

UPSILON

upsilon

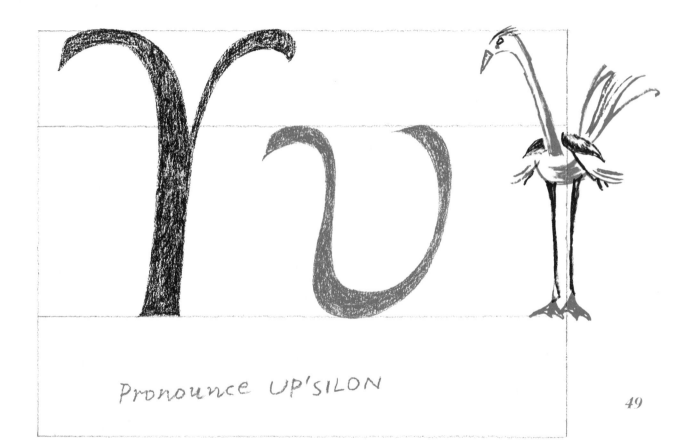

Pronounce UP'SILON

49

PHI is like F.

To write it's a laugh.

Just draw a circle

And cut it in half.

PHI

phi

Pronounce PHEE

51

CHI is another

Kind of Greek K,

But it's made like an X

Confusing, eh?

CHI   chi

Pronounce KEE

53

PSI is pronounced

With the *ps* in *sips,*

Where what really counts

Is your tongue and your lips.

PSI   psi

Pronounce PSEE

55

OMEGA is last.

It's the ancient long O.

From ALPHA to here

Is as far as we go.

OMEGA   omega

57

And now if you wish

To remember them better,

Keep reading the following

Letter by letter.

Alpha	Α α	ΑΛΦΑ	αλφα
Beta	Β β	ΒΗΤΑ	βητα
Gamma	Γ γ	ΓΑΜΜΑ	γαμμα
Delta	Δ δ	ΔΕΛΤΑ	δελτα
Epsilon	Ε ε	ΕΨΙΛΟΝ	εψιλον
Zeta	Ζ ζ	ΖΗΤΑ	ζητα
Eta	Η η	ΗΤΑ	ητα
Theta	Θ ϑ	ΘΗΤΑ	ϑητα

Iota	I ι	ΙΩΤΑ	ιωτα
Kappa	K κ	ΚΑΠΠΑ	καππα
Lambda	Λ λ	ΛΑΜΒΔΑ	λαμβδα
Mu	M μ	ΜΥ	μυ
Nu	N ν	ΝΥ	νυ
Xi	Ξ ξ	ΞΙ	ξι
Omicron	O o	ΟΜΙΚΡΟΝ	ομικρον
Pi	Π π	ΠΙ	πι

Rho	$P \varrho$	$P \Omega$	$\varrho \omega$
Sigma	$\Sigma \sigma \varsigma$	$\Sigma \Gamma M A$	$\sigma \iota \gamma \mu \alpha$
Tau	$T \tau$	$T A \Upsilon$	$\tau \alpha \upsilon$
Upsilon	$\Upsilon \upsilon$	$\Upsilon \Psi I \Lambda O N$	$\upsilon \psi \iota \lambda o \nu$
Phi	$\Phi \varphi$	ΦI	$\varphi \iota$
Chi	$X \chi$	$X I$	$\chi \iota$
Psi	$\Psi \psi$	ΨI	$\psi \iota$
Omega	$\Omega \omega$	$\Omega M E \Gamma A$	$\omega \mu \varepsilon \gamma \alpha$